Where the Light Flows In

by Sharon C. Eccleston

Dorrance Publishing Co
585 Alpha Drive
Pittsburgh, PA 15238
Visit our website at *www.dorrancebookstore.com*

ISBN: 978-1-6366-1523-3
eISBN: 978-1-6366-1698-8

Where the Light Flows In

FOREWORD

G*olden fireflies, big green grasshoppers* and alley cats, along with blue hydrangea shrubs and the pink blossoms on the Rose of Sharon trees in the backyards.

These are the visions in my mind of my early childhood memories growing up in Crown Heights, Brooklyn. We had migrated from Central America in 1961, and as the youngest of three girls I was so carefree and catered to. Blessed in a home filled with love, hope and dreams of what would manifest for our family, we were happy. Besides my sisters, I had a wonderful Jewish woman who lived two houses down, who loved to entertain me with coffee cake and juice. Whenever I was allowed, I went to Missy's house (her name was Missy to me) and played with her and her cats. We would laugh and just have a wonderful time. I was fascinated with her hands!! She had porcelain skin with puffy blue veins that I used to touch and poke all the time. She always gave me her utmost attention. That little girl had no concept or concern of the environment. In an earlier time, I had somehow managed to open the front door of my house early one morning while my family was asleep. I walked down the steps and then towards the corner. By the grace of God, there was an Italian shoemaker on the corner. He came out of the store and scooped me up in his arms before I could cross the street, called the police and of course they could easily identify which house I came from. I remember!

As was inevitable, new families eventually came on the block. I made new friends and poor Missy was shamefully abandoned by me, but she always had friends and family that visited her. I remember when Missy passed. So much changed!! The community exploded with families coming from mostly the West Indies and also from other communities within Brooklyn. Most that came had small children, for whom like my parents wanted every good thing life could offer here!

We all became family and formed such a unity that it stands today. Too many names to give, but they came from Jamaica, Barbados, Trinidad, Haiti, Monserrat, Panama, Guyana and the Southern States. We were staggered in age and so there was always the spirit of looking up to and pulling up each other, inclusion and being responsible for each other. We had an unstoppable Block Association, with an awesome President, and so we learned from early how to come together in strength, goodwill and love for ourselves and our community. The Block Parties and Fashion Shows to raise money were serious acts of entertainment for us. No one could tell us that we did not model like Beverly Johnson, nor were the guys as smooth and as debonair as Billy Dee.

We gracefully came out to music by Grover Washington Jr. - Mister Magic, and Satin Soul by Barry White. What do you know about that?We were fierce and unafraid! Much thanks must go to two wonderful women on that block who gave their time, efforts, patience and love to all the children and young teenagers. They coached us on poise and grace, and especially they put up with us. We were never rude or disrespectful because our parents had taught us better, but you best believe...we were a handful!! We had awesome moves and it was then that we became our own female version of the Jackson 5 (6 or 7) for whatever day or event that it was necessary. We all had a skill, a joy and a love for dancing.

Spike Lee makes reference to "the stoop" in his blockbuster *Crooklyn!* Boy, was he on the money with that. He got that so right!! The stoop was the place that we discussed our fears and our dreams! Where we argued and made up! Where we played jacks and of course talked about boys! It was where we entertained each other and engaged in the fantasies of growing up and becoming adults and what we wanted to be! Where we laughed hysterically and sometimes cried! There were so many of us that some would have to sit at the bottom of the stoop, and others at the top and during the day, we would mix it up at some point so that everyone got a piece of the each other for the day. It was where we sat and rested after our games of punchball, handball, Chinese ball and double-dutch, and talked about who did the best. We were never jealous of each other! We knew each other's strengths and weaknesses and we inspired each other. And on the days that the weather was bad, or during wintertime when we could not be on "the stoop," we went into "the basement." That is when we sang and played indoor games. Each one of us fancied ourselves to be that girl in the Temptations' hit song "Just My Imagination"—well, at least I did!

We went from house to house with absolutely no fear. There was a warm visage on everyone's face—our block was special and had such a beautiful soul of its own. Each family reared their own children, but collectively and in unity we reared each other. Somewhere during this time I received my nickname, "Pearl." Till this day, if I hear someone shout that name I would look around expecting to see one of my teenage friends. I remember!

Looking back everything seems so different! The snow seemed whiter and it fell with a grace that was of its own time. The hundreds of Christmas lights during the holidays seemed to come out of a movie theater. On the brownstone houses and apartment buildings the sun and the moon glinted off the surface—it was a time of unrest, but there was a bond that was prevalent throughout our community! The summers seemed like they were longer and lazier. When we got in at night our skin felt like it had soaked up every bit of the rays that our bodies could endure. We showered and slept, and the next day we would be right back at it with the same gusto if not more. I remember!

One day back in the mid-90s I was sitting in the backyard and a silly thought just popped into my mind: Where did all the big green grasshoppers and golden fireflies go? It seemed like eons since I had last seen them. Time had certainly passed, but life was now being celebrated in so many other new ways. They were now just very, very, very different!!

I dedicate this book of poetry to all those with a dream and purpose in their heart and in their spirit! Let nothing stop you, believe in yourself no matter how long ago you felt inspired and felt a need to do, say or become what you were called to. I encourage you to remember those dreams! Be consistent, determined, and focused. Remember how unafraid you were as a child and bring that to the forefront. Whatever gifts, talents, brand or craft you may have, be strong and be intentional about them!!

Give it all you've got, and trust His Light!

Works

They Are Our Jewels

Our jewels we so cherish
from morning, noon and night,
They are radiant, warm and precious
in every possible light

Their hair is gray from root to tip,
but it shines with health and zeal,
Diamonds are they with fire,
with strong and wise appeal

Their eyes maybe a little cloudy,
but they sparkle just the same,
Emeralds of dignity and fortitude,
we have the pleasure to stand and claim

They're just a little sluggish now,
but their hearts beat with pride and love,
Rubies are their bloodline,
they were taught this from those now above

Their hands are now a little aged,
but we remember all that they did for us in the past,
Topaz days of nurture and care,
are stamped in our minds and will last

Their laughter may be a little softer,
but their heartfelt expressions can't be missed,
Sapphire smiles that lift our hearts,
make us grateful that they are still in our midst

Jewels are they in every way,
like **Pearls** we might often display
Priceless gifts that we will treasure,
forever and a day!!

The Bridge

A very old bridge am I,
for hundreds of years here have I stood,
Made by man of mortar and stone,
I stand for the common good

I serve those who live on the right,
and those who live on the left,
Both sides believe the other is the lesser,
both believe they are best

I hear their words as they go to and fro,
so prideful and filled with scorn,
They speak and think in supreme vanity,
and thus cannot be forewarned

Forewarned of the seeds that they sow,
and the fruit that it will bear,
Blind to how they nurture their sons,
sons who will become their heirs

So shall continue for many years,
a pattern wrought with bitterness and hate,
Their reasons rooted in distorted legacies,
twisted and now sadly innate

And though both sides evolve and progress,
in knowledge and technologies,
Challenged are they in wisdom,
for they are oblivious to the Eye that sees

So each will boast and beat their chest,
of their skills and superior ability,
They impress to all their inflated honor,
forgetting that above all is humility

Miss they do, their own striking resemblance
to the foe that they want to subdue,
Right and wrong is so distinct,
but the features of "self" seems always to elude

Their ideologies and platforms for life,
they find so integral and profound,
Yet there is a simpler call to humanity,
even nature knows when to seek higher ground

And as the air fills with tension,
malice and the hearsay of what will come,
It is the prelude to pain and anguish for thousands,
decided by the powerful some

Behind hidden agendas of what is really sought,
and motives that are far worst,
It all comes down that they hadn't a clue,
the order of what to seek first

Many will meet in the air, sea or a field,
to settle what they feel they must prove,
So vain and arrogant are they to dismiss,
the Hand that will surely move

In the end it did not matter whether their cause was bad or good,
nor even wrong or right,
Gone were many who did not understand the magnificence of love,
over power and might

But in the deep shadows of the night,
their spirits walk together without hate or strife,
And in the quiet stillness you can hear them say,
"Why, oh, why could we not have done this in life?"

Revealed to me that is made of stone,
is the unmitigated truth with the blush of each dawn,
Supreme and glorious is the Creator of all,
still the same today as was centuries foregone

From the four winds of the earth blows His master plan,
in all its enchanting splendor,
And the message within is the novel idea, that to Him,
all things must be surrendered

When this mark is met in every mind and soul,
only then can peace and goodwill meet,
For until the response is of the ultimate reverence,
therein will lie man's true defeat

When the goals transform from most powerful and first,
and aspire to loftier measures,
Then shall he walk and be guided by the truth,
that the heart will follow that which it treasures

It Has to Be Okay

I was told a simple phrase today
and it laid like a blanket, secure and warm,
A simple and promising revelation,
and my mind received it and I let it take form

It flipflopped down into my heart,
and in my spirit it unfurled,
"It has to be okay," he had said,
my new mantra for the World

I plugged it into wherever it would fit,
and it made all wrong feel right,
Where there was chaos and things were mess,
I imagined I saw a light

A light with the power that came from the hills,
from the sky and glow of the stars,
And in the glow I saw no persons,
no kings, rulers, leaders, nor czars

To community, to city, to country, to continent and culture,
there will be an intercession that spans,
"It has to be okay," he said,
for there is One who knows the plans

For we all can choose to be concerned for people,
they need not be family or friend,
In fact they can be quite the stranger,

remember that long ago known Samaritan

There is a crisis for us to give care
to those who are unsafe and huddled,
And we will all do well to consider the concept,
of getting into "necessary trouble"

Through our conscience let us be reminded,
that a chance for life should all be bestowed,
"It has to be okay," he said,
for there is One who is the same yesterday, today and tomorrow

As it happens there is the concern
of uncharted and struggling economics,
We look for ways of absorbing the blows,
of what could be terribly astronomic

How will we condense, scale down, make do,
and learn new ways to be content?
And by this resolve we accept,
that our frivolities and fluff will be much less frequent

The goal is to understand the raging decline
and walk through the financial mire,
"It has to be okay," he said,
for there is One who is a great multiplier

And came to be as foreshadowed by history,
a modern-day menace hard to endure,
Many a thought of how it came about,
but what was utmost was the fight for a cure

A threat that perceived no distinctions at all,
cared nothing about geographics, class or race,
And pray as we would to minimize this war's rage,
and then for the full onslaught we braced

That we would learn as best we could
and proceed with all safety, caution and speed,
"It has to be okay," he said,
for there is One that will meet us exactly in our place of need

As we feel the air around us, the heavy that prevails
is the color of one's skin,
There is a hopeful realization that we are at a place in time,
to let real change begin

*N*otorious, *r*epulsive, *b*ias, *g*rievous deeds
are what we want to forever eradicate,
By Divine mercies we are still standing,
thankful for our strength and traits

Disparities, hate and inequality,
we cannot be lukewarm if we want progress,
"It has to be okay," he said,
for there is a Purpose in the Process

What has happened? There is something amiss—
The seasons and climates have changed,
The seas, the land and polar bears
are mysteriously becoming so strange

The trees and forests are burning, hurricanes coming by twos—
there is an unseen link,
The Black Panther and animals in the rainforest,
we don't want them to become extinct

Emissions pollute the environment all around us,
for our breathing it is quite unfit,
"It has to be okay," he said,
for the earth is the Lord's and all that is in it

A civil right it is,
and the highest of our nation's democratic staple,
To vote is an inherent articulation of our voice,
and to hinder this is simply shameful

With unbelieving eyes we astutely perceive,
the appalling attempts of suppression,
A tool that sustains us with a measure of dignity—
our ultimate societal expression

Never will we surrender this right,
From our ancestors this is our legacy and mandate,
"It has to be okay," he said,
for there is One who will make the crooked places straight

Bewildered we seek that which is strong and mighty,
and it can be such a spiritual search,
Sweetly we whisper that perhaps there is a Rock,
such as the Body of a faithful Church

Let us look to the benefit of hindsight that this 2020 has brought,
in spite of all we have endured,
Surely we have new perspectives, forgetting condemnation
and welcome truth and love at the door

With hope we will look for rainbows,
for the beautiful sparkling days, iridescent and smooth as satin,
"It has to be okay," he said, for There is One Who Gives
Immeasurably More than We can Ask or Imagine!!

Breath

There is an intricate life force and this is no happenstance,
To sea life, mammals, animals, and insects in the sand
Giants and fairies, not one exception to its utter reliance,
And most especially, epically, irrevocable to Man

A gift bestowed by the One who is threefold,
Of this, there is no possible ambiguity
Matchless to be sure, no replication nor mold,
For this, there is the most absolute certainty

A testament to the power and depth of what is unseen,
It is a precious commodity, and the constant victor over death
From the time that we became aware, now and in between,
The master common denominator, is the incredible gift of Breath

Can it be mimicked? I think not at all so,
Could it be harnessed in some inexplicable way?
Can it be contained or reserved for the future as if in escrow?
No impossible, for without it you will not live to see another day

Man can architect a hundred-story building
to collapse within a precise perimeter,
She can calculate a spaceship's speed, time and place,
to safely reenter Earth's exterior
He can make new legs out of titanium
as the daily status quo,
We unbelievably defy gravity every day,
behind the genius of lift and flow

To operate on a fetus within the womb,
this is not a problem.
Transplant most organs,
and if any complications we can likely solve them

Separating conjoined twins in all probability
will be a great success,
Masterfully perform surgeries on delicate brain
and aneurysmal illness

We can pluck relics from the ship at the bottom of the sea,
ill-fated on her maiden voyage,
Make agricultural genetic modifications in size,
and also reduce spoilage

Tell what will appear in the sky up above,
predict the next blood moon,
Create cinematics and film techniques,
so grotesque we could verily swoon

We can manifest these herculean and miraculous feats,
but not the sanctity of Breath,
There is no scientific, medical, nor magical simulation—
of this we are quite inept

So honor the magnificence and give deference
in how we pay homage to its respect,
Let us never, ever serve and wield it in a power
that is evidently disproportionate

It is the ultimate requirement
that keeps us alive and able,
The very last thing that doctors
battle for on the table

And although resuscitation is quite possible
and can be done,
Make no mistake that immortal wind,
comes to us but from One

What you cannot give,
you surely cannot take,
I hear my grandmother,
as she spoke this to us for our very sake

Our ego and psyche need not be hyped
to some superior imagination,
Let us forever change,
treat each other with Love and look to our Creation

Out of our hearts stem the issues of life,
what we daily inhale and exhale,
For the weight of our deeds and our tolerance of others,
there is a mighty scale

Remember that what will count most
is not so much your former acts, but your latter,
And so what we do up until our last breath,
assuredly is what will forever matter

I KNOW GANGSTA

How do we embody this concept,
what is it that we perceive?
Maybe there is something not quite copacetic,
maybe it's a depiction not to be naïve

Some may say a little underhanded,
just plain wrong, or not the most ideal,
A little character flawed, villainous,
or maybe tunnel vision to their options that are real

Shady, rogue and cunning can all fit here too,
a determination to win or to simply survive,
As opposed to strategic, tactical, unwavering—
all different views of how one stays alive

Sometimes it's not immediately apparent,
but we are not shocked when the veil slips,
You can then quickly shift your interaction,
and their agenda you can eclipse

Other times we would have to be senseless,
To miss just who is standing or sitting before you,
The shift of their eyes, the play of their hands,
body language that undeniably exudes

Yet still there are others with a subtle mystique
that you can sense, intoxicating to be sure,
And though every signal tells us that we need to resist,

there is a very captivating allure

While another is purely in for the psychological game,
seasoned in the battle of control and will,
They are looking for a worthy opponent,
to hone and to then master their skills

The last is the one most astounding indeed,
one you thought you had a clue of their capabilities,
But here is someone you perceived to be flat and harmless,
to whom you never saw their possibilities

Now you look at them with new eyes,
and remember all the things you thought were unintentional,
You blink, focus, and now it becomes clear,
that this person is quite multi-dimensional

Can the concept of nature vs. nurture be summoned here,
could it really be just that simple?
Do we learn Gangsta or draw from our inclinations,
when to masquerade and flash the deadly dimples

To understand with a keen second sense,
the most advantageous presentation and timing,
Then to orchestrate, focus and then set up,
the best scenario or disguise for the priming

What you may never understand is the reason
or the cause of what is driving this ruse,
You will have to play this out and try to mitigate,
the outcome of their intentional misuse

And if we all could be honest,
there is one or maybe several things about us that are true,
Maybe we should all just stop, reflect and see,
that every single one of us, has Gangsta in us too

No, no, don't be upset, I speak of Gangsta not of Sinister—
that which is much darker and ominous,
But intrinsic to "we" is a space within where bad wins over good,
and of this we must be cognizant

Most thankful are we that forever will be,
something much greater than the Gangsta within us,
Though rarely deserved,
we can be at peace with a graceful promise that we can trust

And if we dare unfold this further,
we can be certain there is One who knows Gangsta too,
The truth is that He whispers to you even now, "
I knew you in your mother's womb"

And He does not use the word Gangsta for us as we do,
but in love He calls us "Broken,"
And as we walk, live and learn,
let us take the time to understand these words as spoken

For that which may be tainted and bruised,
we can still salvage the good that is inside,
Someone's Gangsta may not be your cross to bear,
but its essence in us all cannot ever be denied

THE GLANCE THAT SEES

The glance that sees is not necessarily covert,
it can pick up nuances quite by accident,
What is revealed can be knowledge indeed,
a confirmation or a blessed enlightenment

The key here is to believe that there is a distinct purpose,
there will come eventual understanding,
Accept what it brings, be still and allow for your growth,
new wisdom and for expanding

We know that life brings many twists and turns,
and the universe responds to our spirit and energy,
Many times this glimpse is specifically for your benefit,
be open and allow for that synergy

Some say there are no coincidences,
that we are in alignment with time and space,
You could have been somehow absent or detained,
but you were destined to be in that exact place

Your move now is to construct your discipline,
consider how to inspire yourself and to aptly proceed,
And when you do with all diligence,
make sure to embody your faith and creed

Understand that if for nothing else,
this has played a part in your needed transition,
You are further equipped to continue on,
but you are aware that there will be more editions

Be not anxious for the future,
don't you worry if you are in the presence of friend or foe,
Hold on to the fact that you are not to be concerned,
for there is One that sits High but looks Low

FOUR SISTERS AND ONE BROTHER

There were several who stood before us,
but it was five that reached in and pulled,
The expectancy of extraordinary touched us,
and the sanctuary was blessedly full

When the first opened her mouth and spoke,
we knew what she was asking us to do,
And so we contritely stopped pointing fingers,
and minimized our saintly views

She was not rude but to the point,
The **CHURCH** should embrace, love, teach and correct,
To lead and transform the believer and the lost,
it is the original plan for the desired effect

The second spoke about the wellsprings in our lives,
the ones we draw from called **FAMILIES,**
Whether core or extended, love and care should abide,
she rebuked dysfunction and anomalies

She said in these relationships we should share secrets and dreams,
give access to our innermost space
To have concern and consideration for them daily,
and hope and pray this trust never be misplaced

Let the little ones and the youths sit front and center,
let their ears and eyes never miss a beat,
They must have a rich reservoir to draw from,
yes, when we are able, put them in that seat

Then the third stepped up and the momentum increased,
her gift to us was **COMMUNITY,**
How does one walk each day in mindless immunity,
and miss countless needs and opportunities

Said she, there are concerns and issues where we can be used,
to be part of the evasive solution,
We must go out of our way to make sure that to all,
there is a fair and empathetic distribution

That our golden jewels who are still here,
can live out their twilight years safely and with dignity,
To enable our little ones to step into their gifts and future,
there must be unwavering equality

When the fourth lifted her mic and calmly walked forth,
something told me she had much to share,
There was a maturity in her eyes that defied what I perceived,
that she appeared youthful in her lived years

I thought to myself, how could she know the intensity and security,
of the joy and bliss of **BLIND FAITH,**
But in complete transparency she told of her painful woes and hurt,
told us of her past trials and fate

Though a soldier in her battles, she proclaimed it was Him
and only Him that brought her safely through,
And we who heard never doubted her testimony nor conviction,
that she knew that which she knew

The fifth was so unassuming in his attitude and stance,
there was the faintest of smiles on his lips,
We would never have suspected that what he came to minister to us,
was on the power of **LEADERSHIP**

He said thoughts and words must be carefully communicated,
for when expressed they are far reaching,
They set the stage for accountability led by example,
and must always be evident and forever in keeping

When the vision is clear a leader makes it plainly understood,
and he is committed to the end,
His heart should be brave, and up for any fight,
but in wisdom and for peace, his hand will he extend

Honesty will make others comfortable to follow him,
and his integrity will take that comfort higher,
And as long as his confidence never resembles arrogance,
he will continually be able to inspire

The ambiance that followed when all five finished,
left no doubt we had received a word in season
The praise and cries that came to our mouths,
was beautiful and filled with a divine reason

As we filed out in the aisles we knew all that we needed to share,
and all that we needed to keep,
Spirits lifted we walked into the night knowing in our hearts and minds,
that deep had called to deep

As I Walked

As I walked, there were carefree days,
filled with winsome times and frolic,
Endless laughter, tricks and pranks,
much happening that was without logic

As I walked, I was surrounded to my left and right,
in front and in back of me,
Noise and excitement within and without,
so very much to do and to see

As I walked, I had to hear all the chatter,
I could not afford to miss one thing,
I wanted to always be on the inside looking out,
never on the outside looking in

As I walked, my choices were shaped
by the fads of the day and times,
There was little thought and even less care,
to contemplate and to reason the signs

As I walked, caution though present,
was layered with curiosity, ego, and daring,
Most times my agenda was to impress or align,
rarely to consider the full bearing

As I walked, I took a look at the world,
and all that I could obtain and acquire,
Such prospects, ambitions, and opportunities ahead,

but what would that all require?

As I walked, I missed a step, I fell and
from the inside was black and blue,
That which was steady and sure before was altered,
and now all things were new

As I walked, life's texture changed,
it was no longer a caress that would glide over me,
What once covered me like flowing silk,
now felt as coarse as the bark of a tree

As I walked, great oceans formed,
gulfs separated me from places and spaces I once knew,
Drops of salty water could attest to my disillusion,
but the great majority had not a clue

As I walked, I talked a lot less than I remembered,
introspection became my art,
What touched me now I could barely understand,
not sure when this happened nor the start

As I walked, patience and calm magically appeared,
a gift that became a new norm,
A quiet learning to be sure, it guided me safely
through deep valleys and many storms

As I walked, my thoughts of the what,
the why and the how now constantly persisted,
Ironically the answers came not from the outside
but from within,

it seems I had it twisted

As I walked, I became aware of the drift of snow,
its symmetry and how it fell down,
A deeper awareness of all that was around,
a different sense of feeling and of sound

As I walked, my movements expressly changed,
and I now let my breath out slowly,
No longer harried or hasty; brash or assuming,
but now walk in a gait that sustains me wholly

As I walked, my ear heard the wind say
what it surely could have not, “Go to the right or go left”,
And as I went forth I had an uncanny notion,
that I had just taken part in some unknown test

As I walked, I came face to face with humanity and seasons,
life’s natural ebb and flow,
And then the dawning came into my mind, body and spirit,
the One to whom I owe

As I walked, I smiled anew
and embraced this evolving coherence,
Discerning that I would never know why,
I was touched by this wonderous perseverance

As I walked, the days beckoned with hope,
and prayers went up on wings at night,
And after many turns my feet found a narrow path,
laid beautifully and bathed in light

I Am Well

We woke one morning and felt a deep void,
yes, a shift had taken place,
A light in our lives that sparkled so bright,
had left its earthly space

And so for some time we were all bewildered,
and lost in our pain and shock,
But then realization and understanding came,
and it was as if it opened a lock

No longer were they here in our world,
where we could see their sweet face and talk,
But they now hold the hand of our heavenly "I Am,"
and together they are on that glorious walk

We found our breath once more in that,
and gave "Thanks" for every single beautiful year,
The memories are precious and they give us strength,
but we know there will always be tears

But in quiet times and when we are very calm,
there is a subtle vibration in the air,
We feel their warmth and know that they smile,
and are helping us through this struggle we bear

And deep within our spirit we hear,
an audible expression that we just cannot dispel,
It is soft, warm and flowing,
and it says to us simply "I Am Well"

So we say to you who are holding us up in friendship,
faith and love – as our hearts swell,
They are around us in other forms,
and they say to tell you … "I Am Well"

The Little Red Cardinal

My thoughts were so distracted as I started getting out of the car,
Though my body was present, my mind was busy with life, and was so very far

Then of a sudden I saw just above my head, something that seemed quite erratic,
A fire-colored little bird had landed on a line, with such drama and acrobatics

There was a full leaved tree just feet away, I believe that was his intended destination,
However, he seemed to dismiss it and doubled back, to sit and give me his bold consideration

He was a scruffy little thing, and looked like he just hopped out of a bird bath barely dried,
Twitched he did as he looked down at me, cocky and sure like he was some mystical guide

I smiled and that seemed to meet some accordance with him, it was then that he started to sing,
"Listen to me" is what he seemed to say, take heed to the melodic counsel that I bring

Let me tell you what I have discovered as my little wings have taken me from east to west,
Open your mind to all that I have to impart to you . . . . .and so, I stood still and acquiesced

He said dominion you were given, pay it forward with the gravity it deserves,
Make the right choices and life will surely flow, select what must be preserved

Great fear and aggression have I felt, deliberate dishonesty and division,
Think not only about yourself, but for others provide the selfless provision

Make the move; don't wait to be asked, you were created to do good works,
Measure and balance what it is you effect, be wise with the posture and power that you exert

Do not amass your valuables on earth, send your treasures heaven bound,
Listen and watch closely where you tread, be careful of the world made crown

Embrace and love who you were made to be, fit in your skin like a glove
You will build on your own self-worth, and it will keep you standing when push comes to shove

Lead with compassion and kindness, have a healthy respect for life's depth and brevity,
Let your presence bring an instant smile to others, exude the warmth of truth, joy, and levity

With that he twitched once more and turned, it seems he had conveyed all that he needed to say,
And there came a breeze that caught his little wings, and he abruptly just flew away

As if in a daze I shook my head, and watched the departure of this tiny red feathered minstrel,
It was then I noticed the atmosphere had changed, it was now filled with specks of sparkle and tinsel

What did it all mean I pondered carefully, and then the answer came in focus as in 3D imagery,
That all five inches of him perched precariously, on a thin wire line . . . was complete in simple **Dignity**

Kiwi, Blueberries, and Walnuts in a Pink Bowl

The phone rings, and there is a deadline at hand
that you already know you can't possibly meet,
You answer carefully, grateful for your skill in diplomacy,
to the caller you respond and entreat

There are choices to be made, a pile of mail on the sofa,
and there's your only black shoes that need soles,
A myriad of concerns but then you take notice,
of the Kiwi, Blueberries, and Walnuts in a Pink Bowl

There is an elation when you look upon the essence of Source,
there is a ***Reset*** that takes place inside,
You see an array that is symbolic of an inexhaustible power,
given to you in ample supply

Sweet and tart is the kiwi, much like life and
one of nature's laden power pack of health
Mightier than many ailments of concern,
greater than any imagined or real wealth

A textured brown skin that is as rich as the earth itself,
a wood found choice that fits,
Soft but firm and brilliant green inside,
with tiny black seeds for that needed grit

A compact oval that fits perfectly into the niche of your hand,
its branch a mastered design,
Inside down the middle a radiant halo from top to bottom,
its stem connected to the faithful vine

A small but perfect orb is the blueberry with a five-point star crown,
a majestic look of its own,
A harness of sustenance greater than other fruits,
one hundred times larger when full grown

Five elements are said to be embodied here, earth, air, fire, water
and spirit, allow yourself the indulgence,
Let its commanding blue color of wisdom intoxicate you,
let your soul delight in the abundance

A neutralizer at the most fundamental level,
with a human and holistic connection,
There is a balance inherent that we can benefit from,
in this tiny circle of infinite protection

Now there's the canopy of trees with clusters of outward fruit
with a seed called the walnut deep inside,
A hard shell covers and safeguards that chambered brittle-like flesh,
twin halves are found in the divide

Wellbeing to your body and nourishment to your bones,
it's truly a metabolic prize,
A booster that is easy, light and gratifying;
a selection that is most assuredly wise

A supporter of our internal processes,
circulation from the heart, veins and skin,
It's a great choice for your overall challenges,
it's a sure enough way to win

Now allow what seems ordinary to shift your perspective,
may your eyes truly comprehend what you see,
Let your subliminal juxtapose you to the extraordinary,

to fruits of the spirit from a benevolent trustee

Taste the goodness and let joy spring up inside you,
let those looming mountains become gentle knolls,
Let trepidation, despair, or the trifling offense be diffused,
using your self-control reduce the rising gall

Eat from this humble vessel, be present and grateful
for its purpose now being used in time,
Absorb the mix and all that it carries,
for it is the stamina and forbearance for your trek and climb
Feel the faithful calm and patience given,
know there is an ever-present help that will never be denied,
Enjoy this *"simple happy"*, and understand it to be the truth,
just as sure as August follows July

Note the brilliant pink of this bowl is anything but plain,
there is a euphoria when looked upon that spreads,
Then imagine some mundane and lifeless color,
infused with the most glorious and reverent of all reds

There is peace and sufficiency in the most basic,
where we can get a glance of the wonders at work in our soul,
Examine the kindness and charity before you,
and know that restoration can take place from a fruit-filled bowl

From the Balcony

A unique place suspended in air,
between what is above, and below,
A vantage point where you feel and sense,
a subtle but invisible flow

There is an expansion to your peripheral,
which picks up breadth and depth,
It allows you to muse the notion,
of where the super and the natural intercept

Feelings of immunity seem to drift around,
within and through you too,
What can reach you here is limited,
and those who can elevate are few

The shadows seem to dance about,
or is it the lighting which enhances the theme?
But below they seem to loom and lurk,
impeding your reach and dreams

Although it is understood,
that distance bears no relevance to Him who is on high,
Here am I encouraged for I am closer to the source,
that whispers to me…try!

Words, sounds and thoughts come to me,
and form ribbons that filter through my mind,
Whether they bring hope, joy or pain,
the process is always touched by a spirit that is kind

The way I walk is a little different here,
there is a sway that feels inherently air bound,
But the sureness you feel under your feet,
leaves no doubt that you are on solid ground

My stance when still is balanced and poised,
yes, you feel something akin to special,
And if you should dare to close your eyes,
you could imagine this space quite celestial

When you sit there is an aura that surrounds you,
there's a feeling of relaxed ease,
It is so sublime and humble to the point,
you feel like you are on bended knees

There is an element of sustainment that I feel,
a support in time and presence,
A rhythmic pulse that is warm and encouraging,
an essence of a love wholly pleasant

At a distance I make out there's a way up ahead,
everything will be beautiful in its own time,
There's a balm I smell in the air around,
and I know that tomorrow the sun will surely shine

Here it is believable miracles can happen,
nothing is impossible is what is being said to you,
Inhibitions has no place here,
you open your heart and mind and rise to take your cues

Promises are remembered, the haze that obscured
is drawn away on swift and gentle wings,
Your soul is engaged and you align with your core,
that you came from Queens and Kings

Everything is illuminated, colors all around you
extinguish the sullen darkness,
In full circle every season of life comes together,
liberating you with freedom and starkness

Here is my crag in my mountain,
where I can get a glimpse of my destiny and all its tenacity,
It's a place to be quiet and draw from the sweet
and from the bitter, all this I get…from the Balcony

The Gift of Friendship

Many a gift are there in this life, fortunate and happy are we,
Opinions of what they are may vary from person to person
But Friendship is a favored one that most all of us would agree

It is relevant in every facet of our lives, the need of its power is deep,
When we know that there is one that will invest in us
There is a comfort within that we have no doubt we can keep

The Gift of Friendship is steadfast in every circumstance,
It encourages during the darkest of times
Never does it waiver, it is there for the drama and the dance

The Gift of Friendship brings clarity when we face confusion,
Was there through all your hard times,
Witnessed your evolution

The Gift of friendship is always loyal, committed and sympathetic,
Light within your spirit
Ageless, timeless, has no geographical limits, and can even be telepathic

It bears witness to that phone call that is reluctantly made,
On any given day
The response is "I'm coming! I'll be there to give you aid"

The Gift of Friendship engages, challenges, and respects you too,
It is considerate of all your concerns
Here you get safe advice, here is where you can talk, spill, and spew

It chuckles at misunderstandings and arguments, rebukes contention,
Embraces forgiveness
And then wishes you a life full of blessings, with absolutely no pretention

It is the color of the purest shimmering gold,
Refined during the fires
With not a smell of smoke, a wonder to touch and behold

And when the tears of life comes for whatever the reason, season,
Occasion or event, that Friend is right next to you or in tow
An extension of all that you are, and all that you are feeling,
And they are picking up the pieces and letting you know . . . .

I got you, from your head down to your toes!

The Beauty in the Desert

I came upon a desert once, its stillness was so deep,
Such isolation did I feel that my soul began to weep
Engulfed in a world of obscurity where my eyes could see no end,
Frozen in my vulnerability, nothing with which to defend
The heat I felt was merciless, the rays scorched more than skin,
My heart and mind felt branded from a senseless pain within
And so I walked by some strange force for how else would I know,
How to navigate the quickening sand, powdery and white as snow
My feet were pulled and sucked down upon, but struggle I did not,
I knew some how to relax and let go, and was freed from a spiraling lot
Filled with dread of what could hurt me, close or far no matter the size
Creeping, crawling, on two or four, would it be apparent or in guise

The darkness brought another dimension, my fears of what I could not see,
Yet worse of all would it be something that I could never, ever conceive
How did I get here? That was where my mind would often stray,
But something deep inside responded, No, ask how long will you stay?
Such a lost state was I, that I fell down unto my knees,
I counted every ragged breath, I only got to Three
It seemed so long before I stood, my stance now having shifted,
But then again I am not quite sure, it felt more like I was lifted
And then it came a breeze so soft that I thought it was imagined,
It kissed my brow and danced over my face, dispersing every margin
And so I inhaled long and sweet, and such a fullness came over me,
But even sweeter was the release, the exchange making me light and free

Like dew a damp mist touched my skin, so refreshing and supreme,
It felt divine and wonderful, like the spray from springs or streams
My eyes seem to focus now, I can see palm trees in my midst,
They stand in humble defiance, that here they could exist
Looking to the heavens at night a thousand stars,
and all their promises I embrace,
Then I look down to behold miles of velvet sand, and I see undulating grace
No earthly coordinates do I have for you, no directions can I give,
But from this desert you will find your way out, sustained by a spirit to Live
You need not look back; it is in your mind's eye, no need to be unsure,
Trust where guidance has brought you, led by Love and all that which is pure
Yes, there is beauty in the desert, be open to its Wisdom and you will receive,
For it can transform your Fears to Faith, and bestow the ability to
BELIEVE!

Be Still and Know That I Am God

Psalms 46:10